Gilbert & Sullivan for Singers

Mezzo-Soprano

Edited by Richard Walters

To access companion recorded accompaniments online, visit:
www.halleonard.com/mylibrary

4669-5454-2288-8118

Cover illustration: W.S. Gilbert created line drawings to accompany his librettos. His childhood nickname was Bab (derived from "baby"), and this was the name he signed to the drawings. They have become known as the "Bab Illustrations." From *HMS Pinafore*, Captain Corcoran and a stylized Little Buttercup are shown at the Captain's lines, "Ah! Little Buttercup, still on board? That is not quite right, little one."

ISBN 978-0-634-05943-8

Visit Hal Leonard Online at
www.halleonard.com

Contact Us:
Hal Leonard
7777 West Bluemound Road
Milwaukee, WI 53213
Email: info@halleonard.com

In Europe contact:
Hal Leonard Europe Limited
Distribution Centre, Newmarket Road
Bury St Edmunds, Suffolk, IP33 3YB
Email: info@halleonardeurope.com

In Australia contact:
Hal Leonard Australia Pty. Ltd.
4 Lentara Court
Cheltenham, Victoria, 3192 Australia
Email: info@halleonard.com.au

W.S. Gilbert

Arthur Sullivan

Contents

Because this role may be sung by either soprano or mezzo-soprano, the song is included in both volumes of the series.

Pianist on the recordings: Laura Ward

The price of this publication includes access to companion recorded accompaniments online, for download or streaming, using the unique code found on the title page.
Visit **www.halleonard.com/mylibrary** and enter the access code.

Plot Notes

THE GONDOLIERS
or *The King of Barataria*

First produced at the Savoy Theatre, London, on December 7, 1889 for an initial run of 554 performances. Twenty-four Venetian flower girls are arranging the bouquets they will present to Marco and Giuseppe, the handsomest of all the gondoliers, in hopes of snagging a marriage proposal. The gondoliers decide to choose their brides via a game of blindman's-buff. Happily they end up with the girls they most wanted—Marco with Gianetta and Giuseppe with Tessa. A gondola arrives carrying the Plaza-Toro family. The penniless Duke of Plaza-Toro tells his daughter, Casilda, that as a baby she was married by proxy to the infant son of the King of Barataria. (Casilda loves the drummer Luiz.) The King's Grand Inquisitor objected to the monarch's religious practices, so he kidnapped the infant prince and took him to Venice to be raised by a gondolier. The prince, who does not know he is a prince, is now himself working as a gondolier in Venice. The court of Barataria has all been killed, and this gondolier is now king, if he can be found. The two newlywed couples return, with Tessa singing **"When a Merry Maiden Marries"** in nuptial celebration. The Grand Inquisitor is certain that one of the men, Marco or Giuseppe, is the King he seeks, although he can't say which, and takes them both back to Barataria. They will rule jointly until the King's old nursemaid, who is the mother of Luiz, can determine which is the real King.

Act II opens in the Court of Barataria, where the democratic leanings of the joint Kings are immediately apparent. The Kings toil all day for their kingdom and they miss their brides. The brides appear, unable to bear the separation any longer. When the Grand Inquisitor arrives, he explains that this sort of thing had been tried once before to no good end. The Duke arrives with Casilda, who is technically married to one of the two Kings, and Luiz. The three brides ponder the predicament of their two husbands and Casilda's mother sings **"On the Day When I Was Wedded,"** telling of her own marriage. The Grand Inquisitor brings in Inez, the nursemaid, to identify the real King. She confesses that when the King was kidnapped she tricked the Grand Inquisitor by substituting her own son. One of the "Kings" is the son of the gondolier Palmieri, the other is the son of the nurse-maid Inez, and the rightful King is Luiz! So the two Kings are gondoliers once again, each happily married to his love. Luiz, now the rightful King, and Casilda happily must be married.

HMS PINAFORE
or *The Lass that Loved a Sailor*
First produced at the Opéra Comique, London, on May 25, 1878, with an initial run of 571 performances.

On the *Pinafore*, anchored off Portsmouth, the crew is proudly polishing and scrubbing the vessel as this satire on British class distinctions and military life opens. A woman named Little Buttercup comes aboard to sell them ribbons and lace for their sweethearts, introducing herself with **"I'm Called Little Buttercup."** Despite her merry demeanor, she carries a mysterious secret. Sailor Ralph Rackstraw, the smartest man in the fleet, declares his love for a young maiden. That maiden, unfortunately, is the Captain's daughter. The sailor Dick Deadeye appears with the unkindly explanation that Captains' daughters do not marry mere sailors. Enter the Captain. He explains to Little Buttercup that he is worried because his daughter, Josephine, has refused to marry Sir Joseph Porter, First Lord of the Admiralty. Josephine herself enters, declaring her love for a sailor aboard Pinafore. After her father explains the class issues involved with her romance she promises to forsake the sailor and reconsider Sir Joseph. Ralph finally summons the courage to confess his love to Josephine, only to have her respond coldly. A heartbroken Ralph threatens to shoot himself, but Josephine relents and confesses that she indeed loves him.

As Act II begins, the Captain paces the deck by night. He confesses his love for Little Buttercup but quickly explains that their different social positions make a relationship impossible. Little Buttercup cryptically advises him not to be too sure of that. Sir Joseph and Josephine enter. Sir Joseph is convinced that Josephine is intimidated by his high social standing; all the while she plots her elopement with Ralph. The evil Dick Deadeye informs the Captain of Josephine's upcoming elopement, allowing the Captain to stop the marriage. The crew steps in on Ralph's behalf, but the Captain curses at this behavior, which brings Sir Joseph out of the woodwork to berate him for speaking so rudely to a British sailor. Once Sir Joseph realizes his love intended to elope with Ralph, he orders the young sailor confined below decks. At the last moment Little Buttercup brings out the truth of her mysterious secret. Apparently she once worked as a nanny of sorts, and made a terrible mistake through which two babies were mixed up. Those babies were the Captain and Ralph. So, in fact, the Captain is a mere sailor and Ralph is the Captain. Her news rings in a happy ending, as Ralph and Josephine, as well as the Captain and Little Buttercup, are freed from social restrictions and may marry.

IOLANTHE

or *The Peer and the Peri*
First produced at the Savoy Theatre, London, on November 25, 1882, with an initial run of 398 performances.

The lovely fairy women of Arcadia are unhappy in this satire on the House of Lords, because the Fairy Queen has banished Iolanthe for marrying a human. The Queen, who is secretly in love with a human named Private Willis, eventually relents and pardons Iolanthe. Iolanthe returns, looking like a young woman of 17 even though she has a 25-year-old son. Her son, Strephon, is planning to marry Phyllis, the young ward of the Lord Chancellor. But the couple has not received his blessing. The Lord Chancellor and a chorus of nobles march about demanding respect and fanfare. The Lord Chancellor loves Phyllis himself, but fearing the marriage would not be proper he asks the nobles if one of them might marry her. Phyllis announces her objection, adding that her heart has already been given to another. Strephon enters at that moment and announces that he is the object of her affection but the Chancellor dashes his hopes. When Strephon tells his mother of these goings-on, she takes him in her arms to comfort him. Phyllis sees Strephon in the arms of this apparent 17-year-old. Certain she has been betrayed, she becomes engaged to two noblemen. As the act comes to an end, the Fairy Queen decides to send Strephon to Parliament to make nobles out of commoners and generally make life miserable for the Lord Chancellor and the other nobles.

Act II opens on the Westminster Palace Yard. Strephon has caused an uproar in Parliament, whimsically passing pointless laws. The peers appeal to the fairies. They offer no help but find the peers quite attractive. Despite her love for Willis, the Fairy Queen sings **"Oh, Foolish Fay"** to scold them for even thinking about marrying mortals. Phyllis meanwhile finds her two fiancées equally uninteresting so she tells them she will choose the one who will forsake his title and give his wealth to the Irish tenantry, which neither will do. Strephon eventually convinces Phyllis that Iolanthe is really his mother and they plan to marry immediately. The Lord Chancellor has in the meantime convinced himself that it be acceptable for him to marry his ward. But Iolanthe steps forward to plead for her son, singing **"My Lord, a Suppliant at Your Feet."** Iolanthe then confesses that she is the Lord Chancellor's long-lost wife. The Queen is about to order Iolanthe's execution for this marriage, when the fairies step forward to announce they have all married nobles. To save them all from execution, the Lord Chancellor rewrites the law so that any fairy who does not marry a mortal will be condemned to death. The Queen happily marries Private Willis to save her own life. Wings sprout from the nobles' shoulders as the House of Peers becomes the House of Peri.

THE MIKADO
or *The Town of Titipu*

First produced at the Savoy Theatre, London, on March 14, 1885, with an initial run of 672 performances. The setting for this most popular of Savoy operettas is the courtyard of the Japanese Lord High Executioner in the town of Titipu. Handsome Nanki-Poo, a wandering minstrel, runs in looking for the lovely Yum-Yum. He has loved Yum-Yum for a long time and now that Ko-Ko, Yum-Yum's guardian and fiancée, is to be beheaded he sees his opportunity. However, Ko-Ko has been reprieved, and enters to announce his new appointment as Lord High Executioner. As he discusses his wedding plans, Yum-Yum and two school-mates enter. Nanki-Poo apologizes to Ko-Ko for being in love Yum-Yum, receiving forgiveness. Later, Yum-Yum confesses to Nanki-Poo that she does not love Ko-Ko. Nanki-Poo confesses that he is actually son of the Mikado and is traveling in disguise to avoid marrying an elderly woman who mistook his good nature for affectionate advances. The Mikado meanwhile has sent word to Ko-Ko that if he doesn't execute someone soon his title will be abolished and the town reduced to a mere village. Ko-Ko spots Nanki-Poo about to end his life over his hopeless love, and asks if he might execute him since the lad is about do himself in anyway. Nanki-Poo agrees on the condition that he be allowed to marry Yum-Yum and live with her for one month before the execution. Ko-Ko agrees, being a more practical than romantic man. When Katisha, the elderly woman who wants to marry Nanki-Poo, arrives and tries to tell everyone of his true identity, she is ignored.

Act II opens on the preparations for Yum-Yum's wedding. Obsessed with her own beauty, she wonders why she should be so much more attractive than anyone else. But happiness dims when Ko-Ko learns that by law she, as the widow of Nanki-Poo, must be buried alive following his execution. A bribe to the Pooh-Bah (also known as the Lord High Everything Else) to fake a certificate of execution seems the best course of action until the Mikado arrives. When Katisha sees the execution certificate and tells the Mikado that his son has been executed, the Mikado promises punishment to all involved. Ko-Ko goes to Nanki-Poo for advice. Nanki-Poo advises him to marry Katisha. Katisha curses her own existence in the dramatic **"Alone, and Yet Alive."** Ko-Ko woos her with the tale of a dicky-bird that died of a broken heart, and soon the two join in duet and then in marriage. Nanki-Poo, now free from Katisha's clutches, comes out of hiding and introduces the Mikado to his new daughter-in-law and thus ends the threat of punishment and the operetta.

PATIENCE
or *Bunthorne's Bride*
First produced at the Opéra Comique, London, on April 23, 1881, with an initial run of 578 performances.

A bevy of lovely maidens are gathered at Bunthorne's Castle as this satire on the aesthetic movement opens. All of the maidens are smitten with the poet Reginald Bunthorne, who has secret feelings for Patience, the village milkmaid. Only Lady Jane realizes the truth of his affections. Patience wonders why people in love never look quite healthy, so the maidens explain that they have always been in love. In fact they were once engaged to the Thirty-Fifth Dragoon Guards, who immediately march on stage followed by their Colonel. But they are no match, in the maidens' eyes, for poet Bunthorne. Bunthorne himself enters, seemingly engrossed in a poem he is composing but slyly listening to everything. As he reads his poem aloud the maidens become even more smitten with him. The Colonel reflects upon how he used to think a uniform would make a man irresistible. Bunthorne soliloquizes, explaining that he is an aesthetic fake. He then makes romantic overtures to Patience, who is not interested in love. But the maidens explain to Patience that love is a duty and she decides to fall in love. Another poet, Archibald Grosvenor, arrives and proposes to her. He reminds Patience that he is the boy she had loved as a child. Bunthorne, meanwhile, has decided to raffle himself off, only to be stopped at the last minute by Patience's offer to marry him. She indeed loves Grosvenor, but believes that she can only love unselfishly if she has no feelings for the object of her affections. The maidens decide to turn their affections back to the Dragoons, only to redirect them to Grosvenor the moment he appears.

As Act II begins, Lady Jane is deciding to forsake the Dragoons in favor of Bunthorne. She feels that they ought to marry in a hurry, explaining with **"Silver'd Is the Raven Hair"** that she is not getting any younger. Grosvenor enters, with the smitten maidens traipsing along behind, making it clear that his heart remains with Patience. Patience now realizes that she should be with Grosvenor whom she loves, but duty requires that she keep her promise to marry Bunthorne. The rival poets are wildly jealous of each other by this point. Bunthorne demands that Grosvenor cease being an aesthetic and Grosvenor eventually agrees. Bunthorne decides to reform his unpleasant traits. Patience decides that loving the now perfect Bunthorne is hardly unselfish, so she feels free to love Grosvenor, who has become a common-place, everyday man, as per his agreement with Bunthorne. Lady Jane and the maidens all marry Dragoons, leaving Bunthorne alone with his false poetry.

THE PIRATES OF PENZANCE
or *The Slave of Duty*

One performance, for copyright purposes, was given on December 30, 1879 at the Royal Bijou Theatre in Paighton, Devonshire. It opened officially for a run in New York at the Fifth Avenue Theatre on December 31, 1879. The London premiere was at the Opéra Comique on April 3, 1880, with an initial run of 363 performances.

Pirate festivities on the Cornwall coast open this satire on British military and constabulary, celebrating the completion of young Frederic's pirate internship. But Frederic is dejected. His situation is explained by Ruth, who had been his nursemaid, with **"When Frederic Was a Little Lad."** It seems that Ruth, being quite hard of hearing, mistook Frederic's father's instruction to apprentice him as a pilot and instead set him up as a pirate. The heartbroken Frederic must, for duty's sake, return to the honest world and work to end piracy even though this means betraying his pirate friends. He begs the pirates to give up their life of crime but they decline. Ruth begs Frederic to take her with him, as he has never seen another woman and considers the aging Ruth to be beautiful. Just then a party of beautiful young maidens appear for a picnic and are shocked to find a pirate in their midst. He pleads with them to take pity on him. Just when it appears that all will reject him, Mabel appears and bravely offers him her heart. The other pirates spot the lovely maidens and creep in to kidnap them. The girls' father, the Major-General appears, hoping to foil the pirates' plans of marriage. He plays on his knowledge that Pirates of Penzance are orphans and are always tenderhearted toward other orphans, explaining that he too is an orphan and would be lost and lonely without his daughters. The pirates relent and the Major-General, Frederic and the girls depart, leaving poor Ruth with the pirates.

Act II opens in a ruined chapel, where the Major-General confesses to Frederic and Mabel that he is not actually an orphan. Frederic explains his plans to put the pirates out of business, and is in the process of proposing to Mabel when policemen arrive on their way to conquer the pirates themselves. They are just describing their grand plans when Ruth and the Pirate King arrive with a most ingenious paradox. Apparently Frederic was born on a leap-year day, so he won't actually reach his 21st birthday until 1940. Therefore he is still the pirates' apprentice. Always a slave to duty, Frederic returns to his pirate life, where honor forces him to tell the pirates that the Major-General is not an orphan. The policemen reappear and reluctantly prepare to arrest the pirates. The pirates meanwhile can be heard sneaking up on the Major-General. Just as the pirates are about to do in the Major-General, the policemen leap to his defense, only to be defeated almost immediately. They are about to be killed when the police pull

Union Jacks from their pockets and command the pirates to stand down in the name of Queen Victoria. The pirates, who love their Queen, comply. Ruth puts everything to rights by explaining that the pirates are actually noblemen who have gone wrong. They are immediately forgiven and given back their titles. Frederic and Mabel reunite and the Major-General asks the pirates/nobles to marry his daughters.

PRINCESS IDA

or *Castle Adamant*
First produced at the Savoy Theatre, London, on January 5, 1884, with an initial run of 246 performances. *Princess Ida* is the only three-act operetta by Gilbert and Sullivan.

This satire on women's suffrage and Darwin's evolutionary theories opens on a scene of great expectation. Prince Hilarion awaits the arrival of Princess Ida, to whom he has been betrothed since infancy. But her father, King Gama, arrives without her, explaining to the Prince and his father King Hildebrand that Princess Ida is now running a school for girls at Castle Adamant. There they study the classics and the villainy of men. Hildebrand and Hilarion decide to hold Gama and his three sons as hostages while they storm the Castle Adamant to claim the Princess.

At the Castle Adamant, Lady Psyche, Professor of Humanities, instructs her students that man is ape at heart, in **"A Lady Fair of Lineage High."** Lady Blanche, Professor of Abstract Philosophy, declares that she was born to be a ruler, in **"Come Mighty Must!"** Hilarion and two friends scale the castle wall and disguise themselves in women's clothing. With several of the women aware of the men, and keeping their secret, the three pull off the ruse for a time. But after drinking a bit too much, one of the men gives up the secret. Princess Ida orders the men's arrest. But King Hildebrand has massed his troops outside the castle walls to force Ida to make good on the betrothal. He gives her twenty-four hours to make up her mind, threatening to raze the castle and hang her brothers and father if she declines.

The Princess decides to fight, but her students are in terror of hurting someone so they refuse. Meanwhile King Hildebrand has decided that fighting women is in poor form, so he has Ida's brothers brought from his castle to fight for the women against Prince Hilarion and his two friends. Hilarion and company win. Princess Ida marries Hilarion, and two of her colleagues marry his friends. Lady Blanche is left to fulfill her dream of running the school and the curtain falls.

RUDDIGORE

or *The Witch's Curse*
First produced at the Savoy Theatre, London, on March 14, 1885, with an initial run of 288 performances.

The professional bridesmaids in the Cornish village of Rederring are antsy for work. The lovely Rose Maybud is the most likely candidate, but she keeps rejecting suitors. She explains that she is waiting for the right person. Rose's Aunt Hannah tells of Sir Roderic Murgatroyd of Ruddigore, her lost love, and sings of the history of the curse of the Murgatroyd heirs in **"Sir Rupert Murgatroyd."** Roderic defied the curse, which condemns the Murgatroyds to commit a crime each day or perish, and died on their wedding day. Despard Murgatroyd has assumed the title and is living the obligatory life of crime. The shy Robin Oakapple, who is really Sir Ruthven Murgatroyd, appears. Robin explains that he is too shy to approach Rose. Robin's half brother, a sailor named Richard, offers to woo Rose on Robin's behalf, but falls madly in love with her and woos her for himself instead. When Robin learns of this betrayal he poisons Rose's mind against sailors and she turns her affections to him. At this point Mad Margaret enters, singing **"To a Garden Full of Posies,"** and **"Cheerily Carols the Lark."** Driven to insanity by her passion for Despard, she is wildly jealous of Rose, who reassures her. The plot thickens when Robin reveals himself as Despard's older brother, whom all thought was dead. Robin's title is restored and Rose leaves him for Despard. But Despard spurns her, going back to Margaret. Rose returns to Richard and Robin collapses.

Act II opens with a haggard Sir Ruthven (Robin) in the picture gallery of his castle, looking for a crime to commit. Rose and Richard have come to ask permission to marry and Ruthven threatens to imprison Rose as his crime of the day. Richard pulls out a Union Jack, which of course even the worst of criminals cannot ignore, and the two leave safely. At this point the portraits of the previously cursed Murgatroyds come to life to remind Ruthven what will happen if he fails to commit a crime. Ruthven wearily sends someone off to kidnap a maiden on his behalf, which brings Hannah to the castle. In the meantime Despard and Margaret, now school masters, arrive to encourage Ruthven to reform. They add that under the law Ruthven is responsible for Despard's crime as well as his own. Ruthven vows to reform, no matter what the consequences. With Hannah in the room, Ruthven calls upon the picture of his Uncle Roderic to help him. Roderic's picture comes to life and he spots Hannah. Ruthven leaves, contemplating his predicament. But the day is saved when Ruthven rushes back in with a brainstorm. Failing to commit a crime each day while knowing the sentence for such action is death, he reasons, is tantamount to suicide. Since suicide is a crime in and of itself, Sir Roderic should never have died. This means that all concerned may pair off as they see fit and thus ends the curse and the operetta.

UTOPIA LIMITED
or *The Flowers of Progress*
First produced at the Savoy Theatre, London, on October 7, 1893, with an initial run of 245 performances.

This mockery of Victorian society is set on the fictitious South Pacific island of Utopia, where the King's daughter, Princess Zara, is about to return from school in Britain. Two wise men, Scaphio and Phantis, hold power over Utopia and its King. The two wise men tout their own virtues. Tarara explains that as the Public Exploder he must explode anything or anyone denounced by Scaphio and Phantis. A scandal sheet called the *Palace Peeper* has accused the King of terrible behavior and Tarara thinks it is time for an explosion. The King announces that due to public demand Utopia will be modeled after Great Britain, with Lady Sophy teaching the girls proper behavior. We learn that the King himself has written the scandal sheet, under orders from Scaphio and Phantis. Scaphio has promised Phantis to help him win Zara's heart, but one look at her and he is in love with her himself. Zara and Fitzbattleaxe interrupt, explaining that in Britain if two men love one woman they must duel to the death to decide who wins the woman. The King tells Zara of Scaphio and Phantis' power over him. She has conveniently brought "experts" from England to set Utopia to rights. As per their advice, the King incorporates himself. In fact, everyone in Utopia is now a limited company.

Act II finds the King dressed in British military attire, ready to hold his first cabinet meeting. With Scaphio and Phantis grumbling about the Anglicization of Utopia, the King tells them he is a limited company and therefore immune to their control. They call in the Public Exploder and cook up a plot. Lady Sophy reveals her feelings for the King, singing **"When But a Maid of Fifteen Years."** The King tells Lady Sophy the truth about the *Palace Peeper* and about Scaphio and Phantis. But things are now too good in Utopia. There is no work for the Army or Navy, no disease for doctors to cure and no crime for lawyers to prosecute. So the King decides to follow the British system of Government by party saying, "No political measures will endure, because one party will assuredly undo all that the other party has done."

THE YEOMEN OF THE GUARD

or *The Merryman and His Maid*

First produced at the Savoy Theatre, London, on October 3, 1888, with an initial run of 423 performances.

The year is fifteen-hundred-and-something. Young Phoebe Meryll ponders the heartbreaks of love, singing **"When Maiden Loves, She Sits and Sighs."** She is pining for the dashing Colonel Fairfax who sits in the Tower of London awaiting execution for the crime of sorcery. He was accused of the crime by his scheming cousin. Should he die without a wife, Fairfax explains to the Lieutenant, his title and wealth transfer to the cousin. When Phoebe launches a verbal assault on the Tower for its excessive bloodletting, Dame Caruthers, the housekeeper to the Tower, sings **"When Our Gallant Norman Foes"** in defense of the "sentinel." Fairfax begs the Lieutenant to marry him to the poorest woman that can be found so that she might inherit his name and wealth instead. Jester Jack Point and singer Elsie Maynard enter. A less than appreciative crowd threatens to mob them but the Lieutenant saves them, immediately marrying Elsie to Fairfax. Meanwhile, Phoebe has come up with a plan. She flirts with Wilfrid, Head Jailor and Assistant Tormentor of the Tower of London, singing **"Were I Thy Bride."** She steals his keys just long enough for her father to free Fairfax. Wilfrid is barely gone when Fairfax appears in the uniform of the Yeomen of the Guard, posing as the son of Sergeant Meryll. As Phoebe and her "brother" give each other an uncommonly affectionate greeting, the bells toll the hour of the execution. Guards rush back with the news that Fairfax has escaped.

Act II finds Jack Point feeling regret for allowing Elsie to marry Fairfax. It seemed a better idea when Fairfax was about to die, since Jack wanted to marry Elsie himself and figured Fairfax's money would be welcome. He advises Wilfrid on the hazards of jesting. The newly freed Fairfax is putting the fidelity of his new wife to the test, masquerading as Leonard Meryll. Jack and Wilfrid conspire to fake Fairfax's death, saying that they shot the Colonel as he dove into the river. With Fairfax thought dead, Jack proposes to Elsie, who rejects him. Fairfax wonders who his new bride might be, only to discover moments later that his bride is Elsie. Phoebe, distraught over loosing Fairfax tells Wilfrid of the escape and disguise. Wilfrid forces her to marry him to keep the secret. Suddenly the real Leonard appears with an official pardon for Fairfax. Elsie, at first heartbroken to learn that her real husband is alive is delighted when it is revealed that her beloved Leonard is really Fairfax and therefore they are married. Jack, the only one left without a spouse, falls to the ground in a faint.

Gilbert & Sullivan for Singers

Mezzo-Soprano

When a Merry Maiden Marries

THE GONDOLIERS

Words by W.S. Gilbert
Music by Arthur Sullivan

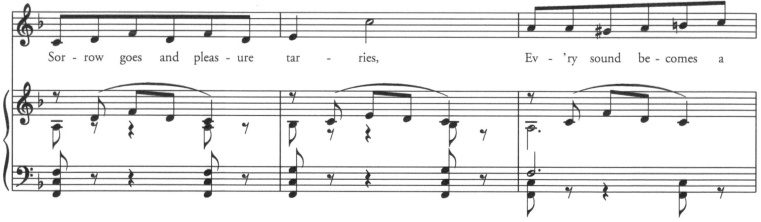

When a mer-ry maid-en mar - ries

Sor-row goes and pleas-ure tar - ries; Ev-'ry sound be-comes a song All is

right and noth-ing's wrong. Gnaw-ing Care and ach-ing Sor - row

Get ye gone un-til to-mor - row; Jeal-ous-ies in grim ar - ray, Ye are

things of yes - ter - day! When you mar - ry mer - ry maid - en,

rall.   *a tempo, sostenuto*

Then the air with joy is lad - en; All the cor - ners of the earth Ring with

a tempo

mu - sic sweet - ly played, Wor - ry is mel - o - dious mirth, Grief is

p

joy in mas - que - rade; Sul - len night is laugh-ing day _____

On the Day When I Was Wedded

THE GONDOLIERS

Words by W.S. Gilbert
Music by Arthur Sullivan

Allegro con fuoco

DUCHESS:

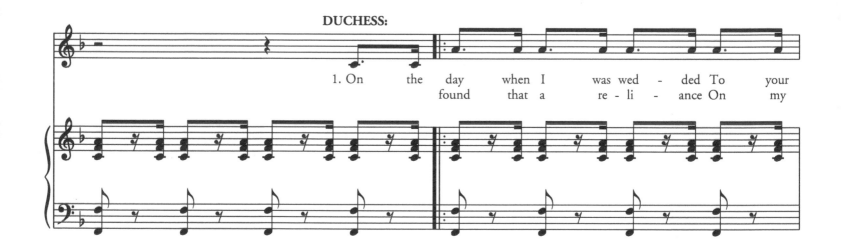

1. On the day when I was wed - ded To your
found that a re - li - ance On my

ad - mi - ra - ble sire, I ac - know - ledge that I dread - ed An ex -
threat - en - ing ap - pear - ance, And a res - o - lute de - fi - ance Of mar -

plo - sion of his ire. I was o - ver - come with pan - ic— For his
i - tal in - ter - fer - ence, And a gen - tle in - ti - ma - tion Of my

tem - per was vol - can - ic, And I did - n't dare re - volt, For I
firm de - ter - mi - na - tion To _____ see what I could do For to

feared a thun - der - bolt! I was al - ways ver - y wa - ry, For his
wife and hus - band too, Was the on - ly thing re - quired _____ For to

fu - ry was ec - stat - ic— His re - fined vo - cab - u - la - ry Most un -
make his tem - per sup - ple, And you could - n't have de - sired A more re -

how   I tried   to tame   your great   pro - gen   —   i - tor—
tamed   your in - sig - nif - i - cant   pro - gen   —   i - tor—

at   first!
at

2. But   I

last!

My Lord, a Suppliant at Your Feet

IOLANTHE

Words by W.S. Gilbert
Music by Arthur Sullivan

Andante non troppo lento ♩ = 76

He loves! If in the by-gone years Thine eyes have ev-er shed Tears— bit-ter, un-a-

vail-ing tears— For one un-time-ly dead— If, in the e-ven-tide of life,

Sad thoughts of her a-rise, Then let the mem-'ry of thy wife Plead for my

boy— he dies! He dies! If fond-ly laid a-side In

some old cab - in - et, Me - mo - rials of thy long - dead bride Lie,

dear - ly trea - sured yet, Then let her hal - low'd

bri - dal dress— Her lit - tle dain - ty gloves— Her

with - er'd flow'rs— her fad - ed tress— Plead for my boy— he loves!

f   *p*   *pp*

Oh, Foolish Fay
IOLANTHE

Words by W.S. Gilbert
Music by Arthur Sullivan

1. Oh, fool - ish fay, Think you, be - cause His brave ar - ray My bos - om
2. On fire that glows With heat in - tense I turn the hose Of com - mon

thaws, I'd dis - o - bey Our fair - y laws? Be - cause I
sense, And out it goes At small ex - pense! We must main -

When Frederic Was a Little Lad

THE PIRATES OF PENZANCE

Words by W.S. Gilbert
Music by Arthur Sullivan

I'm Called Little Buttercup

HMS PINAFORE

Words by W.S. Gilbert
Music by Arthur Sullivan

Allegretto

BUTTERCUP:

I'm called Lit - tle But - ter - cup,

dear Lit - tle But - ter - cup, Though I could nev - er tell why, But

Alone, and Yet Alive
THE MIKADO

Words by W.S. Gilbert
Music by Arthur Sullivan

Silver'd Is the Raven Hair
PATIENCE

Words by W.S. Gilbert
Music by Arthur Sullivan

When Time, grown wea - ry of her heart-drawn sighs, Im - pa - tient-ly be - gins to dim her

eyes! Com-pelled at last, in

life's un - cer - tain gloam - ings, To

wreathe her wrin - kled brow with well - saved "comb - ings," Re -

When But a Maid of Fifteen Years

UTOPIA LIMITED

Words by W.S. Gilbert
Music by Arthur Sullivan

LADY SOPHY: *Recit.*

Oh, would some de - mon power ____ the gift im - part To quell my o - ver - con - sci - en - tious heart— Un - speak the oaths that nev - er had been spo - ken, And break the vow that nev - er shall be bro - ken!

1. When but a maid of fif - teen year, Un - sought— un - plight - ed—
2. Each morn - ing I pur - sued my game (An ear - ly ri - ser);

Short pet - ti - coat - ed— and, I fear, Still short - er sight - ed— I
For spot - less mon - archs I be - came An ad - ver - ti - ser. But

made a vow, one ear - ly spring, That on - ly to some spot - less king, Who
all in vain I search'd each land; So, king - less, to my na - tive strand Re -

proof of blame - less life could bring, I'd be u - ni - ted. For I had read, not
turn'd, a lit - tle old - er, and A good deal wi - ser! I learnt that spot - less

long be - fore, Of blame - less kings in fai - ry lore, And thought the race still
King and Prince Have dis - ap - pear'd some a - ges since— E'en Pa - ra - mount's an -

flour - ish'd here— I was a maid of fif - teen year! Well, well— Well,
ge - lic grace Is but a mask on Na - ture's face! Ah, me! Ah,

well— I was a maid of fif - teen year!
me! Is but a

mask on Na - ture's face, on Na - ture's face!

8ba

A Lady Fair of Lineage High

PRINCESS IDA

Words by W.S. Gilbert
Music by Arthur Sullivan

would not do— His scheme fell through, For the

Maid, when his love took for - mal shape, Ex - press'd much ter - ror At his mon - strous er - ror, That he

stam - mer'd an a - po - lo - gy and made his 'scape, The pic - ture of a dis - con - cert - ed Ape.

ff

2. With a

pesante

p

view to rise in the so-cial scale, He shav'd his bris-tles, and he dock'd his tail, _____

_____ He grew mous-tach-ios, and he took his tub, And he paid a gui-nea to a

toi - let club— He paid a gui-nea to a toi - let club— But it

would not do, The scheme fell through— For the

Maid was Beau - ty's fair - est Queen, With gold - en tress - es, Like a real prin - cess - 's, While the

Ape, de - spite his ___ ra - zor keen, Was the A - pi - est Ape that ev - er was seen!

ff

pesante

p

3. He bought white ties, and he

bought dress suits, He cramm'd his feet in - to bright tight boots— ___ And to

start in life on a brand new plan, He christ-en'd him-self Dar - win-ian Man! He

christ-en'd him-self Dar - win - ian Man! But it would not do—

p

The scheme fell through, For the Mai-den fair, whom the

mon-key crav'd, Was a ra-diant Be-ing, With a brain far - see - ing— While Dar-

win - ian man, though — well - be - hav'd, At best — is — on - ly a mon - key shav'd!

Was a ra - diant Be - ing, With a brain far - see - ing— While Dar -

win - ian man, though — well - be - hav'd, At best — is — on - ly a mon - key

shav'd!

Come Mighty Must!

PRINCESS IDA

Words by W.S. Gilbert
Music by Arthur Sullivan

Cheerily Carols the Lark
RUDDIGORE

Words by W.S. Gilbert
Music by Arthur Sullivan

Sir Rupert Murgatroyd

RUDDIGORE

Words by W.S. Gilbert
Music by Arthur Sullivan

Once, on the vil - lage green, A pal - sied hag _____ he roast - ed, And what took place, I ween, Shook his _____ com - po - sure boast - ed; For, as the tor - ture grim _____ Seized on each with - ered limb, _____ The writh - ing dame 'Mid fire _____ and flame Yelled

forth this curse on him:

"Each lord of Rud - di - gore, ___ De - spite his best en - deav - our, Shall

do one crime, or more, Once, ev - 'ry day, for ev - er! This

doom he can't de - fy, How - ev - er he may try, For

should he stay His hand, that day In tor - ture he shall die!" ___ The

proph - e - cy came true: Each heir ___ who held ___ the ti - tle Had,

ev - 'ry day, to do Some crime ___ of im - port vi - tal;

Recit.

Un - til, with guilt o'er - plied, "I'll sin no more!" he cried,

To a Garden Full of Posies

RUDDIGORE

Words by W.S. Gilbert
Music by Arthur Sullivan

Andante ♩. = 69   MARGARET:

1. To a gar-den full of po-sies Com-eth one to gath-er
   nest of weeds and net-tles Lay a vi-o-let, half

flow-ers,   And he wan-ders through its bow-ers Toy-ing with __ the wan-ton
hid-den,   Hop-ing that his glance un-bid-den Yet might fall __ up-on her

ro-ses,   the wan-ton ro-   ses,   Who, up-ris-ing from their
pet-als,   up-on her pet-   als.   Though she lived a-lone, a-

beds, Hold on high their shame - less heads With their pret - ty lips a -
part, Hope lay nest - ling at her heart, But, a - las, the cruel a -

pout-ing, With their pret - ty lips a - pout-ing, Nev - er doubt - ing, nev -
wak-ing, But, a - las, the cruel a - wak-ing. Set her lit - tle heart

cresc.
_p_

rall.

- er doubt - ing That for Cy - the - re - an po - - sies He would
_ a - break - ing, For he gath - ered for his po - - sies On - ly

dim.
_p_ _rall._

1 _a tempo_ | **2** _(She weeps)_

gath - er aught but ro - ses!   2. In a
ro - ses, on - ly ro -   ses!

colla voce   _a tempo_

Were I Thy Bride

THE YEOMEN OF THE GUARD

Words by W.S. Gilbert
Music by Arthur Sullivan

on thy breast My lov- ing head would rest, As on her nest The ten- der tur- tle dove— Were I thy bride! This heart of mine Would be one heart with thine, And in that shrine Our hap- pi- ness would dwell—

A feath - er's press Were lead - en heav - i - ness To my ca - ress. But then, of course, you see I'm not thy bride!

When Our Gallant Norman Foes

THE YEOMEN OF THE GUARD

Words by W.S. Gilbert
Music by Arthur Sullivan

DAME CARRUTHERS:

1. When our gal - lant Nor - man foes   Made our
2. With - in its wall of rock   The

mer - ry land their own,   And the Sax - ons from the Con - quer - or were
flow - er of the brave   Have per - ished with a con - stan - cy un -

su - ing; There's a le - gend on its brow That is
beau - ty; But the grim old for - ta - lice Takes

el - o - quent to me, And it tells of du - ty _____
lit - tle heed of aught That comes not in _____ the _____

done _____ and du - ty do - ing.
mea - sure of its du - ty.

The screw may twist and the rack _____ may turn, And

men may bleed and men may burn, O'er Lon - don town and its

gold - en hoard I keep my si - lent watch and ward!

O'er Lon - don town and all its hoard,

cresc.

O'er Lon - don town and all its hoard

mf

I keep my si - lent, si - lent watch and ward! si - lent watch and ward! ward!

When Maiden Loves, She Sits and Sighs
THE YEOMEN OF THE GUARD

Words by W.S. Gilbert
Music by Arthur Sullivan

me!" "Ah, me!"

"Ah, me!" Yet all the sense Of el - o-quence

Lies hid - den in a maid's "Ah, me!"